Black Holes

KER THAN

Children's Press®
A Division of Scholastic Inc.
New York Toronto London Auckland Sydney
Mexico City New Delhi Hong Kong
Danbury, Connecticut

Content Consultant
Noreen Grice
Astronomer
President, You Can Do Astronomy, LLC.
www.youcandoastronomy.com

Library of Congress Cataloging-in-Publication Data

Than, Ker, 1980-
   Black Holes / by Ker Than.
      p. cm.—(A true book)
   Includes index.
   ISBN 13: 978-0-531-16894-3 (lib. bdg.)   978-0-531-22801-2 (pbk.)
   ISBN 10: 0-531-16894-8 (lib. bdg.)   0-531-22801-0 (pbk.)

1. Black holes (Astronomy)—Juvenile literature. I. Title. II. Series.

QB843.B55T475 2010
523.8'875—dc22   2008052347

1 2 3 4 5 6 7 8 9 10 R 19 18 17 16 15 14 13 12 11 10   62

Find the Truth!

Everything you are about to read is true *except* for one of the sentences on this page.

Which one is **TRUE**?

T or F   Black holes will one day swallow up everything in the universe.

T or F   Objects that fall into the center of a black hole can never escape.

Find the answers in this book.

Contents

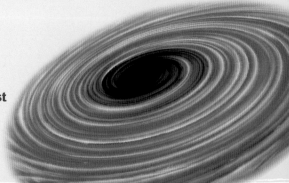

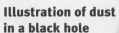

**Illustration of dust
in a black hole**

Centaurus A galaxy

Black holes grow bigger by "eating" gas and dust.

THE **BIG** TRUTH!

Black Hole Jets

Supermassive black hole

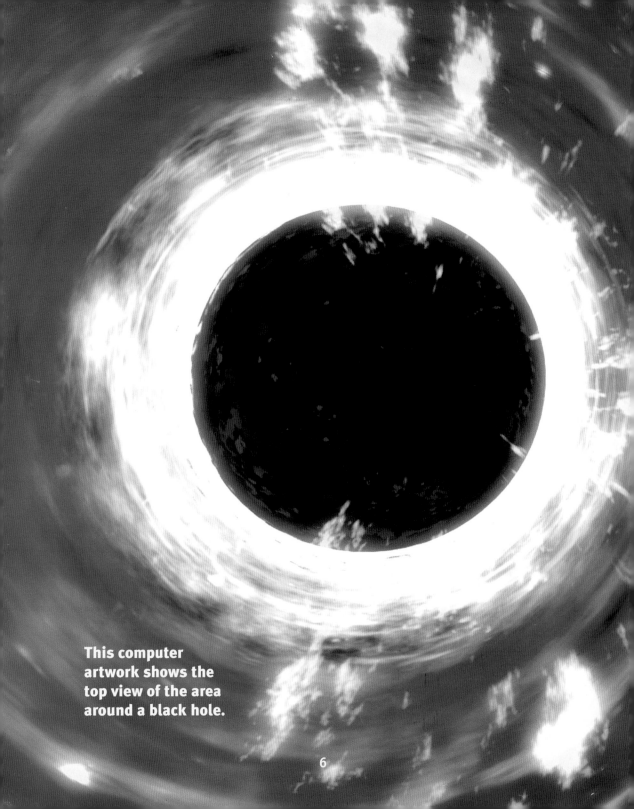

This computer
artwork shows the
top view of the area
around a black hole.

CHAPTER 1

The Dark Side

Stars give off light. That light bounces off most objects in space. This allows those objects, such as planets and moons, to be visible. But there are some objects in space that light doesn't bounce off of and they don't give off their own light either. In fact, they pull in anything that gets close to them, including light. These objects are called black holes.

Black holes were once called "invisible stars."

A Mystery

Black holes are some of the most mysterious objects in space. Nobody knows for sure what's at the center of a black hole. That's because anything that falls into a black hole is lost forever. Scientists know this because even light disappears inside of black holes.

As shown in this illustration, gases from a nearby star can be pulled into a black hole.

Star

Star being stretched

Black hole

Black holes can stretch and pull nearby stars apart.

Both inside and around a black hole, there are forces at work. These forces can pull objects into the black hole or even make them spin around the black hole very quickly. By studying black holes, scientists believe they may learn more about how the universe works.

Some scientists believe that the explosion of star SN 2006GY is the brightest supernova ever recorded.

CHAPTER 2

What Is a Black Hole?

Most black holes in our universe form when very large stars die. These stars can be hundreds of times bigger than our Sun. When the largest stars reach the end of their lives, they can blow up in a powerful explosion called a **supernova**. This explosion is just the beginning of a black hole.

A supernova gives off as much energy in the time it takes to explode as our Sun makes in billions of years.

Blasting Off

A supernova's explosion causes a star's outer layers to blast off into space. At the same time, the star's heavy center or core pulls the rest of the star inward, causing the star to collapse. The collapse is caused by the core's strong gravity. Gravity is an invisible force that pulls objects toward each other.

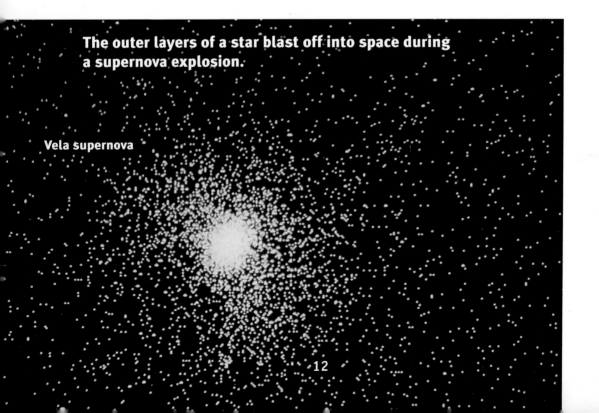

The outer layers of a star blast off into space during a supernova explosion.

Vela supernova

Matter is anything that takes up space. It can be a solid, liquid, or gas. The more matter an object has, the stronger its gravity. The amount of matter an object has is called **mass**. Since very large stars have a lot of mass, their gravity is really strong. After a supernova, a star's core is so compact and its gravity is so strong that the core gets crushed into a tiny point. This makes the star become a black hole.

The Sun has about 333,000 times more mass than Earth. ➡

Earth ——•

Sun ——•

Squished!

Any object could become a black hole if it is crushed enough. If Earth was squeezed down to the size of a marble, its gravity would be incredibly strong. Earth would be a black hole.

Spaghettification

What would happen if you fell into a black hole? It would be a wild ride, but not very much fun. As you got closer to the black hole, its gravity would begin to pull you apart. By the time you reached the center of the black hole, you would be a thin sliver of matter. Since you'd look like a long strand of spaghetti, scientists sometimes call this process "spaghettification."

Before

After

A black hole at the center of a galaxy might look like this.

CHAPTER 3

Types of Black Holes

There are different sizes and types of black holes. From smallest to largest, there are mini black holes, stellar-mass black holes, intermediate-mass black holes, and supermassive black holes. Mini black holes can be smaller than a star. Supermassive black holes have been found in the centers of galaxies. A galaxy is a collection of stars, gas, and dust.

The most powerful types of black holes can be found in the centers of galaxies.

Stellar-Mass Black Holes

Black holes that form from supernova explosions are called **stellar-mass black holes**. Only the biggest stars in the universe can become stellar-mass black holes. Medium-sized stars, like our Sun, are too small to end their lives as this type of black hole. To become a stellar-mass black hole, scientists think that a star must have at least 10–15 times more mass than our Sun.

Stellar-mass black hole

The word stellar means "star."

The star that became this stellar-mass black hole is pulling matter from another star.

Supermassive Black Holes

Another type of black hole is a **supermassive black hole**. These are gigantic black holes that are millions of times more massive than the Sun. Scientists don't really know how supermassive black holes form. One idea is that many smaller black holes join together until they become a single supermassive black hole. The center of many galaxies have supermassive black holes.

Sagittarius A*

Our Galaxy, called the Milky Way, contains a supermassive black hole named Sagittarius A*. The mass of Sagittarius A* is equal to about four million of our Suns. But Earth isn't in any danger from this black hole. That's because Sagittarius A* is a long way off.

The Milky Way

Scientists are studying images of Sagittarius A* like this one taken with an X-ray telescope. They are trying to learn more about how supermassive black holes may be developing at the centers of other galaxies.

With faraway objects like Sagittarius A*, scientists use light-years to measure their distance from Earth. A light-year is the distance that light travels in a year. Since light travels at 186,282 miles (299,792 kilometers) per second, a light-year is about 6 trillion mi. (9.4 trillion km). Sagittarius A* is 27,000 light-years or 160,000 quadrillion mi. (250,000 quadrillion km) away from us.

Mini Black Holes

Although not a mini black hole, this illustration shows what J1650-500, one of the smallest black holes, might look like.

Mini black holes may have the same mass as a comet but still be too small to see with your eyes. A comet is a ball of rock, dust, and ice that travels around the Sun. Some scientists think trillions of mini black holes appeared when the universe was born about 14 billion years ago. Back then, all of the matter in the universe was squeezed into a very small space. Parts of space were packed so tightly that they formed mini black holes. Some scientists think that most mini black holes have disappeared, but some of them might still exist.

Intermediate-Mass Black Hole

Intermediate-mass black holes have masses in between stellar-mass and supermassive black holes. They're sometimes called "middle-weight" black holes. Scientists aren't really sure where intermediate-mass black holes come from. Some think that they are just supermassive black holes that stopped growing.

Scientists have now found intermediate-mass black holes.

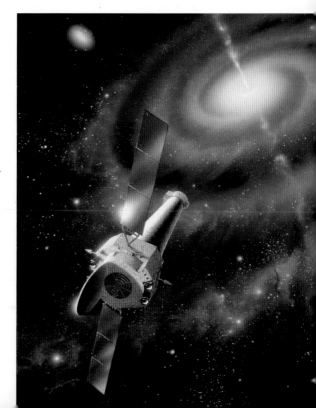

The Chandra X-ray telescope has been used to detect X-rays near black holes.

The Milky Way

CHAPTER 4

Inside a Black Hole

Black holes look like dark empty places in space but they have extremely strong gravity. They come in different sizes and are far away from Earth. While no one has ever seen a black hole up close, scientists have many ideas about them.

Scientists believe that the Milky Way galaxy contains millions of stellar-mass black holes.

Singularity and Event Horizon

Scientists think that at the center of all black holes, a huge amount of matter is crushed into a tiny area. This area is so small that you can't see it—not even with a microscope. Scientists call this area a **singularity**. Nobody knows what a singularity looks like because nothing can go into a black hole and survive.

An **event horizon** is the space around a black hole's singularity where gravity is so strong that even light can't escape. Only objects that cross an event horizon become trapped. Anything outside of an event horizon can still escape—if it travels fast enough. Event horizons are why black holes don't swallow up everything in the universe.

Point of No Return

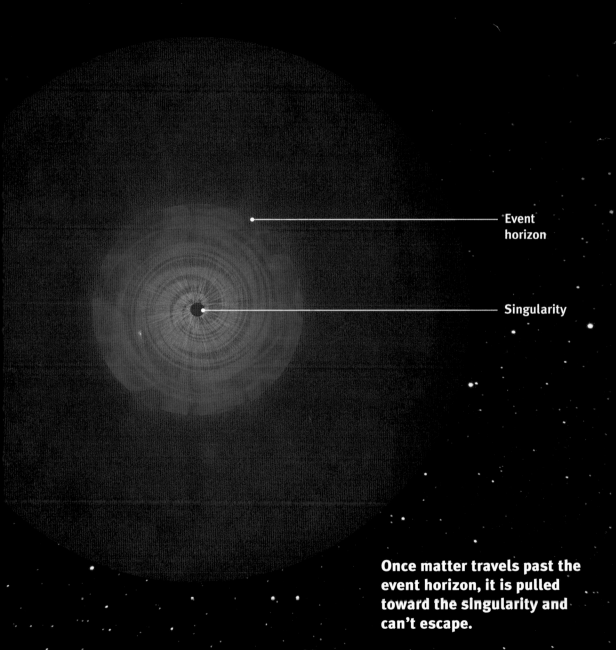

Event horizon

Singularity

Once matter travels past the event horizon, it is pulled toward the singularity and can't escape.

 Some black holes are even big enough to swallow whole stars.

Accretion Disk

Out in space, black holes mostly swallow up gas and dust. But all the matter a black hole sucks up doesn't go straight to the center right away. Most of it swirls around the black hole in a ring called an **accretion** (uh-KREE-shun) **disk**.

Since an accretion disk forms outside an event horizon, much of the matter in it never gets sucked in. It circles around the black hole forever. But the little bit of gas and dust that does get into a black hole makes it grow. As a black hole sucks in this matter, its event horizon gets bigger.

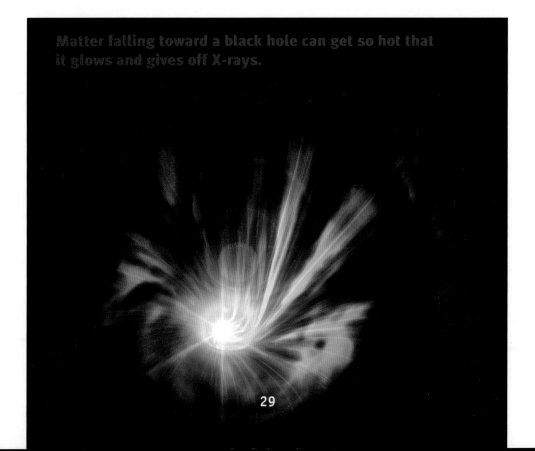

Matter falling toward a black hole can get so hot that it glows and gives off X-rays.

Black Hole Jets

Matter swirling around a black hole's accretion disk can still escape if it hasn't crossed the event horizon. The matter can become shaped into powerful jets by invisible forces around the black hole. The jets are made of very hot gas, called plasma. They shoot out at the top and bottom of a black hole at nearly the speed of light.

Quasars

Quasars (KWAY-zars) are extremely bright and very distant objects in space. Scientists think quasars are supermassive black holes in the center of faraway galaxies. A single quasar can outshine the light of a trillion Suns. A quasar jet can shoot out plasma for trillions of miles.

Matter from a nearby star is pulled into an accretion disk around a black hole.

CHAPTER 5

Understanding Black Holes

Scientists can't look into black holes and study them. Black holes don't **reflect** or give off their own light, so they're invisible to the human eye. But if scientists can't see black holes, how do they know they really exist? One way to study black holes is to watch how they affect the objects around them in space.

The Chandra X-ray Observatory is helping scientists to better understand black holes.

Black Holes and X-rays

If a black hole forms near a star, it swallows gas from the star's surface. But the gas doesn't fall into the black hole directly. It swirls around in the black hole's accretion disk. The gas swirls around so fast that it heats up and gives off invisible energy called X-rays.

The area around this black hole is giving off X-rays. When an object in space gives off X-rays, this is a clue that it might be a black hole.

This NGC 1275 galaxy has a supermassive black hole at its core.

Measuring a Black Hole

Astronomers know a black hole's mass by looking at other objects, like stars, around it. Gravity around a black hole is so strong that it can pull on these objects and make them speed up. The more mass a black hole has, the faster it makes the objects move around it. By watching these objects carefully, astronomers can tell if a black hole is nearby and how much mass it has.

Traveling Through Space

Just like the planets in our solar system travel around the Sun, black holes are pulled toward other space objects by gravity. Two black holes can circle around each other. Over time, they get closer to one another until they combine to form an even bigger black hole.

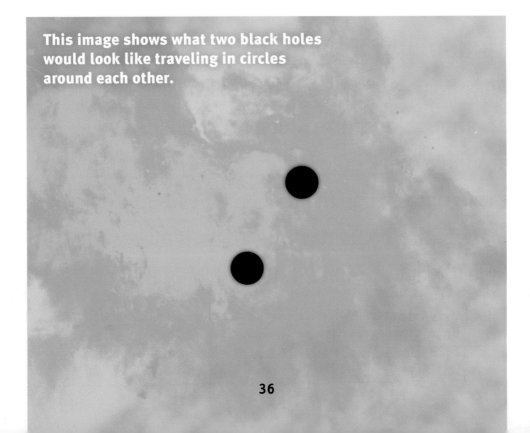

This image shows what two black holes would look like traveling in circles around each other.

Record Breaker

One of the largest known black holes in the universe is an object called OJ287. This supermassive black hole has a mass equal to 18 billion Suns. It's at the center of a quasar that's believed to be 3.5 billion light-years from Earth. Scientists were able to figure out OJ287's mass because a smaller supermassive black hole orbits it. The smaller black hole has a mass that's 100 million times bigger than our Sun.

Footprints in Space

As black holes move around in space, they create gravitational waves. Just as a boat makes waves as it moves through water, gravitational waves are invisible ripples in space created when a black hole or other large space objects move.

Black Hole Milestones

1687 ➡ 1967

Isaac Newton discovers the laws of gravity.

John Wheeler invents the name "black hole."

If an object moves very fast, it creates lots of strong gravitational waves. When black holes combine, they also create gravitational waves. By tracking these waves, scientists can find out information about the black holes that created them. With this information, scientists can measure how big the black holes are and how fast they are circling one another.

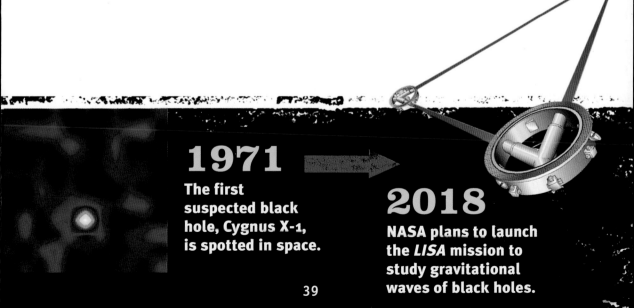

1971

The first suspected black hole, Cygnus X-1, is spotted in space.

2018

NASA plans to launch the *LISA* mission to study gravitational waves of black holes.

LISA Space Mission

Gravitational waves are very hard to find since they're invisible. They also get weaker as they travel further from their source. To help find gravitational waves, NASA and the European Space Agency plan to launch a space mission in 2018 called *Laser Interferometer* (in-tur-fur-AH-muh-tur) *Space Antenna* (*LISA*).

The *LISA* mission will include three spacecraft that will be arranged in a triangle. These spacecraft will be positioned millions of miles apart. They will bounce laser beams back and forth to one another. If a gravitational wave passes through the laser beams, it will change the distance between the spacecraft. Scientists then will be able to locate the waves and try to find out where they are coming from.

The *LISA*

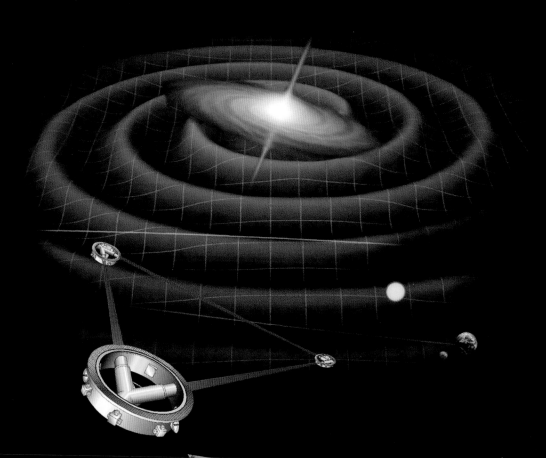

LISA will be sent to orbit around the Sun.

Fascinating Finds

Black holes are some of the most interesting objects that exist in space. Scientists think that black holes hold the key to understanding gravity, the birth of our universe, and much more. With information from high-powered telescopes and X-rays, scientists will continue trying to prove their ideas about black holes. ★

Understanding black holes could unlock many of the greatest scientific mysteries of the universe.

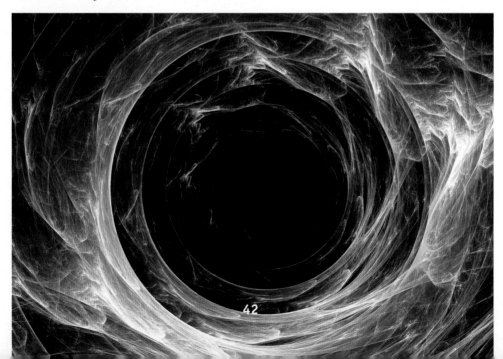

42

True Statistics

The speed of light: 186,282 mi. (299,792 km) per second

Mass of smallest known black hole: 4 Suns

Mass of Milky Way's supermassive black hole: 4 million Suns

Number of stars in the Milky Way Galaxy: Up to 400 billion

Number of galaxies in the universe: More than 100 billion

Distance to nearest supermassive black hole: About 30,000 light-years

Distance to farthest known black hole: About 13 billion light-years

Did you find the truth?

F Black holes will one day swallow up everything in the universe.

T Objects that fall into the center of a black hole can never escape.

Resources

Books

Couper, Heather, and Nigel Henbest. *Black Holes*. New York: DK Children, 1996.

Gore, Bryson. *Astronomy: Every Galaxy Has a Black Hole*. Mankato, MN: Stargazer Books, 2006.

Jackson, Ellen. *Mysterious Universe: Supernovae, Dark Energy, and Black Holes*. Boston, MA: Houghton Mifflin, 2008.

Jefferis, David. *Black Holes and Other Bizarre Space Objects*. New York: Crabtree Publishing, 2006.

Mitton, Jacqueline, and Simon Mitton. *Scholastic Encyclopedia of Space*. New York: Scholastic, 1999.

Oxlade, Chris. *The Mystery of Black Holes*. Chicago: Heinemann, 2006.

Solway, Andrew. *What's Inside a Black Hole?: Deep Space Objects and Mysteries*. Chicago: Heinemann, 2006.

Wright, Kenneth. *Scholastic Atlas of Space*. New York: Scholastic, 2005.

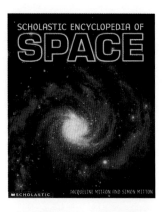

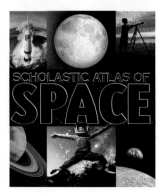

Organizations and Web Sites

HubbleSite: Black Holes
www.hubblesite.org/explore_astronomy/black_holes/
Read more about black holes and take a virtual trip to the ones nearest Earth.

NASA: The Space Place
www.spaceplace.nasa.gov/en/kids/
Visit this kids' Web site created by NASA to learn about space and play games.

Chandra X-ray Observatory
http://chandra.harvard.edu
See black holes in pictures taken by the Chandra X-ray Observatory.

Places to Visit

Mueller Planetarium
210 Morrill Hall, University of Nebraska-Lincoln
Lincoln, Nebraska 68588
(402) 472 2641
www.spacelaser.com
This planetarium projects space movies in a specially designed dome.

Denver Museum of Nature & Science
2001 Colorado Blvd.
Denver, Colorado 80205
(303) 322 7009
www.dmns.org
Explore the Space Odyssey exhibit and visit the fascinating planetarium.

Important Words

accretion (uh-KREE-shun) **disk** – a spinning ring of gas and dust that forms around a black hole

event horizon – the area around the center of a black hole where gravity is so strong that light can't escape

intermediate-mass black holes – black holes with masses between stellar-mass and supermassive black holes

mass – the amount of matter in an object

matter – the solids, liquids, or gases that make up any object

mini black holes – black holes that have about the same mass as large comets

quasars (KWAY-zars) – small, powerful distant points of light that contain a supermassive black hole and shoot out jets

reflect – to bend or throw back waves of light, sound, or heat

singularity – the center of a black hole

stellar-mass black holes – black holes formed when large stars explode in supernovas

supermassive black hole – a very large black hole that is usually found at the center of a galaxy

supernova – a powerful explosion that happens when very large stars die

Index

Page numbers in **bold** indicate illustrations

About the Author

Ker Than is a science writer living in New York City. He has a master's degree from New York University's Science, Health, and Environmental Reporting Program. Before becoming a freelancer, Ker was a staff writer at the science news Web sites LiveScience.com and Space.com, where he wrote about earthquakes, dinosaurs, black holes, and other interesting things.